249

Behind The Closed Door

249

there is a home for all of us.

-z.k.d

i am going to stay here until at least thursday. part of me never wants to leave, but the other part knows i can't sustain a life this way. i have money saved up for it when it happens, but i will need a better structure and plan in place before that begins. i have learned so much about myself these past ten days. i am better this way. i am happier in all phases of my life, even if i am alone out here so to speak. i promise you, if you want it bad enough, the universe will make you work for it, but you will achieve a grand life beyond this one you are living. everything takes time, and with doing so, you value the down time you once thought was a punishment for your past.

i don't believe in a god. i am and have become
more spiritual over the last eight years of my life.
it all changed for me when i got back from
deployment and moved back home with my dad.
i wanted to give my testimony at the church
he went to, and the preacher said it would be okay.
i told them about my suicide attempt and how i had
given up on everything and everyone. my addiction
struggles. it lasted less than ten minutes. after i was
done, i had several people come up to me and try
and shame me, calling me a coward. never have i felt
more like an outcast. after it was all said and done,
there was a girl who was there from a reform school,
who told the preacher i had just saved her life.
before any of this, i asked the preacher if i could
still tell my story, i told him some details and he
almost told me not to. i believe in and speak in
energies. that's what i know. no matter who or what
tries to silence me, my life is more valuable than the
acceptance or judgment from a man of god.

i have ventured out beyond my flesh and discovered a
realness more authentic than before when i thought i
was alive. escaping the cage inside your ribs, is what it
takes to love, to adventure, to be. our thoughts shape
us, so be kind to the feelings being invented upstairs.
most of the time, they are merely passing through.
most of the time, they are just renting out space to
doubt. we are bigger than our fears. we are better
than the troubles we hold in. we need to lean on
the conviction of who who we are in order to live
a meaningful life. if you cannot find kindness in
your heart, may you find it from someone who can.

we ourselves, are the greatest gift to someone else. make sure you are ready to become that for another who needs you. make sure you can be that for yourself before jumping. it is a long way down the rabbit hole if you plan on staying. it is even longer if you plan on leaving somewhere you have known your entire life. before you do make that next jump, know it will kick your ass and make you think you cannot make it. the truest thing we can ever attain in life comes from overcoming the past we make with the devil. after it has come and gone, you will know love exists. you will know love can be given to the most broken of angels looking for a glimpse of heaven to run around in, where things are calm and fruitful for the human underneath its skies.

sometimes the healing comes before you are ready to move on. do not fear the future when the present is still running its course. there is a greatness amongst the believers. there is a wholeness to the lost. there is a loss no one speaks of, but we all know about. these are the steps your lungs take before inhaling. these are the steps your heart takes before learning how to beat wildly for opportunity. we are all wanderers of some distant land, just trying to get back home. even if we do not know where that is, being homesick is not a foreign feeling. it is how we know we are still alive and have yet to find ourselves.

there is a burger king in front of the hotel. a mcdonald's beyond that. a denny's beside me. a black bear diner next to all of them. then the ants come strolling in. they invade at the same time. they leave full and most of the time with leftovers as they get into their cars. it has always amazed me how many people eat fast-food on a daily basis. this world is eating itself to death, but the food industry keeps making it cheaper to attack your heart and veins with the burgers and fries. i enjoy comfort food just as much as the next person, but it is too easy to kill yourself nowadays. we all have our vice; drinking, smoking, love, and food. we all die doing what we love to do. we all are incapable at times of letting go of death to remember what living feels like. if we did, maybe we would appreciate health more than the hangover life hands to us as a daily routine.

i have planted myself in solitude by choice. it has taught me how to deal with my own crisis of being human. of course it gets lonely, but there is a sense of love that rests inside my soul that no one else has ever given to me. until that happens, this sign around my neck remains open for the world to see; i am at odds with who i am and those around me. blooming takes time to love and takes years to appreciate. there is a mystique to being alone and not having someone to care for you. the soil is not always a place for the lonely, but it is there to show us we can become something if we break through the concrete to taste the light. everything above ground reminds us how special of a place this is and how we take for granted the nature we are subjected to. not everything is perfect, but for the small amount of time we are here, it is too precious to ruin what is ours. it is too precious for another shattered heart to be buried without it ever knowing what love is or was or could be.

sitting in this chair, with the door open, has taught me more about who i am than anything i have ever done. all you need to do in order to visualize what you want, is to take in the energy around you and transform it into the steps required to make the door invisible and become one with the land around you. you would be surprised to see how the sun looks at you when you give it time. you would be surprised to see the color of night when you become aware of its powers to heal the cracks in your eyes. you would be surprised how you see yourself once you step into the life that has always been there for you. you might even become someone entirely different than who you are now. i hope you do. i hope you see the love you were born with. i hope you see the love you don't have to accept if you feel it is not being reciprocated. i sincerely hope you do.

i keep walking around this town and find myself constantly inspired by it. the kids playing in the water, splash waves onto my soul. the flowers plant blooms in my bones. the animals bring out the human in me. the weather creates an undying sun in my eyes. the roads are marked and mapped on my hands. i will remember each day as if they were my children; all different. all a part of me. all love and beautiful.

i don't know if i will ever live here, but it will always live within me. places like this don't come to you that often in a lifetime. once you find it, make it a home the best way you can. give it windows. give it shelter. give it a picture of resilience hanging on the walls. when you are ready for this, take a walk outside of it. do not become accustomed to it always being there. our homes are distinct in beauty. give it something inspiring to look at it, and it will never let you down. build it from the inside out. once you are done, repeat those same steps for yourself.

there's a man pushing the trash can out
of the burger king. i wonder what he does
when he gets home? i wonder what he did
before working here? the sun skips across
the pavement as he wheels it out again.
i hope he doesn't always have to do that
for the rest of his life. i hope he finds a
new life to push. i hope he can walk away
into something sacred that is all his own
when he is done with this portion of his life.

one day, nothing will hurt like this. one day, no more tears will fall. one day, love won't feel like thunder splitting down your spine. one day, nothing will matter. but today, i want it all. today, all things take shape in the form of a bountiful pursuit of liberation for the dreams kept shackled to the bedpost of my body. they will know i am sorry for taking so long with freeing what was born free to begin with.
my situations have dictated where i go and who i become. today, i have grown on a mountainside where trees kiss the waterfalls and drink in the sounds of mist forming in the corners of the mouth of darkness.

another quiet day here at the hotel. it's as if i was given the opportunity to scream as loud as i want or need to, yet i am typing them for others to read. we must let it out when we can. it's unhealthy staying calm all the time.

each day brings a new light into my room. each night brings

the moon to my door. each hour brings me a new sense.

each minute brings me a new sound. each second brings me

a new love to give to you.

i went to denny's for dinner. had a fit slam. probably the only schmuck ordering that off the menu. they are at their slowest here between the hours of three and six in the evening. that's when i walk over. i don't mind the crowds here as much as i did before. i guess that's another thing that has changed since being here. but it is relaxing to have the restaurant basically to yourself during your dinner. there were a few people inside. all over the age of fifty. as i paid my tab, this older man paid before i did and held the door for me. as we walked outside i asked him how his day was going after i thanked him for holding the door open.

he laughed and did a double take to make sure he heard me correctly. he said, "i am still alive."

to which i laughed and said the same thing. he was from minnesota. drove a red chevy, and was balding. he seems like he enjoys the solitude as well.

i enjoy not having to answer to anybody. feels like all my life i have been looking over my shoulder, waiting on the next terrible thing to trip me. being here i have only looked forward. more writing. more life. more me. it feels good to be selfish after all. it feels good to take your skin off at a hotel where you are not judged for what you drive or what you dress like. i wish the world could come visit and learn a thing or two of how to be yourself without the rest of the bullshit that follows someone when applying for a better life.

she brings out the freckles on my skin,
makes the goosebumps visible to the stars,
makes me forget to hide my smile and turns
my soul over. she brings out who i try to cover up.
my only wish is to be layered in earth before i ever
feel smothered by my own thoughts of doubt again.

if you're not here to love me, just walk away. my heart has no room left for sheep or cowards. it has no room for a single stride when it is worthy of miles of openness. it has no room for shallow digging when it was meant to be excavated by the one i love. there is no more room available to those who walk in and out as if it were a garage sale with tinker toys being sold. my entirety is vintage and will be appreciated by someone who loves a rustic and patina finish to go along with a sad set of eyes during winter.

i don't know what hurts more, loving someone who doesn't love you or leaving someone that does. i have known both too often in my own life and have come away each time with a new understanding that life will fuck you more than anyone is willing to accept. pain is birthed at the exact time we are conceived. the only way to get through it, is knowing we all suffer during our lives. we all feel the same emotions during the same or different times during the breaths we take and the ones we share. most of the time it will knock you to your knees, you still have the strength to get up and look it in the face and swing as hard as you can until you break open the sky and take what is yours.

sitting here, there goes another second off my life. sitting
here, there goes another thought. sitting here, there goes
the way i was feeling. sitting here, i am earning every day
that comes next, by bleeding out stars and painting
the cosmos on your skin with the words i have kept in,
waiting for someone like you to come by and tell me
you love me as much as i will always love you.

i wonder why it is so easy for those who say they love us to
lie blatantly to our face and behind our back. the question
has been eating at me all week. maybe they are not ready to
take on the full responsibility of loving someone else or
maybe they are and have been this way since they were kids.
whatever the reason is, it's indescribable the pain they can
inflict and the power they have over us as if we are their pet
dog or cat and play and feed us when it best suits them. if i
know anything, it is life will catch them when they least
expect it and make them feel this way when they are actually
ready to give away more than lies. they will grieve the same
loss we have felt, but will never gain a single rose of love,
as they go about taking what was never theirs to begin with.

i became me when i made the choice not to allow others the

ability to control how i felt. once you make it to that point,

life begins opening every door and window you had

previously shut and locked to keep humans away.

i will never believe you or anything that comes out of you. you broke my fucking heart and ruined me. but with all great tragedies, there is victory within. i take from you a lesson to always be vulnerable, no matter how raw the emotion gets. you did your best to kill me, but you only created more fuel to throw into the bonfire. something like that has the power to burn the stars and create a new truth which i will carry with me when defending my wounds. there is no more words for you from me. i have written poetry about the devil, so it makes no difference to me if you ever read these or not. you cannot take back what you did and i will never take back this hatred i have for you at this time or at any point during my life. i will not allow it to manifest past this point, because something as evil as what i feel for you should never be discussed. it just simply is, and will be cast off into the fire where everything dies.

i'm going to take the remaining days i have here and create as much art as i can. it's the only way i know how to live properly. it's my breakfast, lunch, and dinner. it's how i fucking survive.

i have barricaded myself with mountains and lost all sense of time. the only way i can tell time is by counting the key strokes and feeling my back tighten with regret. there is no way out of here, so i will write my way through to the other side where there is sweet relief and immense sunshine for the darkness that followed me into the room. we are not here by choice, but by privilege. once we figure that out, our teeth won't be left to chew on the bullshit.

each day i wait to hear from you and each day i am greeted

with the same silence as the day before. maybe i will learn to

trust my intuition more than the lips of someone beautiful

some day. maybe not all i have loved are soulless. maybe i

have a taste for heartache more than the beginning of love.

when i am not typing, it feels so awkward being alone. my hands fumble anything they touch and they are never filled with certainty. it is a lost art, to be whole without needing anyone. to be happy without needing laughter. to be seen without needing to speak. to love without needing another heart to explain your life story to. during the times of my loneliness, i never reach for someone else. i know nothing can replicate the love i am looking for.

there is only so much a human can take before he or she realizes the lie they have been fed. after that, you've never seen the universe erupt in such a way. sometimes you just have to cut your losses and make it into something worth living and going on about your business without hearing more excuses as to why they couldn't do this or that. it will hurt, but you will be alive to feel someone else be kind and true.

where do the days go when all you asked for was a chance at a new beginning? mine have been spent on making two poetry books and attempting to a build a life out here. one has gone better than the other, but this trip has been a success, because i proved to myself i am able to function and make it without the aid of anyone else. if i can drive twenty-one hours, stay by myself for two weeks, and finish two poetry books, i will make it just fine. we get too caught up in the unknown that we forget about the love that exists in the now. we forget to cherish the next time that may never come.

there was a time last year i was scared to even get in my truck and drive. my anxiety had a rope around my neck and my hands felt like they were cut off. my body would ultimately shut down in thought of leaving the house. it was beyond frustrating and frightening. i was a grown man who couldn't do normal things. i thought i would always be that way. i used to shake before i even tried to open the door and walk out. fast forward to now and i have never been more proud of myself. i am as vulnerable as they come, and being a former infantryman for the usmc, i am victorious because i learned how to overcome and manage this disease. this life sentence for some who sit on death row without hope or a rope to make a getaway.

you were able to hold me and not be afraid of your own

blood. my edges aren't for everyone, but you have sanded

and smoothed my surface. i am glimmering in love.

maybe not all good things come to those who wait. maybe you have to goddamn will it to make it happen. maybe you have to crawl your ass to the finish line. do whatever it takes, because this all ends, and when it does, there is no such thing as regret. it is just you, the box, and dirt.

i can't stand the thought of you being with someone

else. it kills who i am. i just hope you are happy now

and wherever it takes you, i know it is further than i

ever could have.

nothing kills you faster than feeling you aren't good enough

for someone or some thing. you've got just as much reason

as the next to have whatever your goddamn heart desires.

don't let shallow people teach you how to swim.

i was born outside the lines. i was raised by every color the sky has ever presented me. i have sat with the birds. i have rested with the bears. i have climbed with the monkeys. i have flown with the flightless. i have died with the devils. i have lived with sinners and drank with saints. i have watched people pretend to be interested in someone else, only to be fucking someone on the side. i am irony. i am a question. i am a run-on sentence. i am nothing more than the tattoos on my body at times, but at least i show you who i am before the sun rises.

there's a different vibe in the air this morning. it feels like for the first time, things will be okay. it feels like the sun and moon both fell asleep watching the same sunset.

it feels like they are more in love than ever before.

get up, sweet child. knock the blood off.
you are brave enough to try again. let the
rebel out. when all the madness settles,
you're going to look back on this time and
be thankful you didn't give up. this breaking
point you feel is not made to undo what you've
done. it is here for us to finally break through to
the life we deserve.

my mother would wake up and make sure we were ready for school. i would have already been up, but it was comforting to have someone come in to check on you. i didn't have a normal childhood, but she did her best being the mother and father. when i got older, i finally realized what a broken heart could remember and what a soul looked like after being suffocated by fear. i finally understood the late nights by herself in the garage. i finally understood why her breakdown was warranted. love can destroy us if we are open to it being for forever, but it can heal us in the same ways if we are honest with the one we are sharing our sorrows and truths with.

i ruin everything because i have never had anyone care for me long enough to know not all humans hurt each other. some only know how to hurt themselves. i've been more concerned about the well being of others for so long that i forgot how it is to actually feel and care about your own pain.

i walked over to redmond to grab brunch. ordered the avocado toast. first time i ever bought voss water. not too pricey. a little over two dollars. also bought a bottle of kombucha. sat outside and ate. it has become my favorite place here to chill and eat. chase waited on me this time. cool cat and has a good vibe about him. danielle waited on me last time when i had the farm burger. top three burgers ever for me. the toast was sourdough and had a spicy chipolte sauce. just the perfect snack. the voss water was hinted with tangerine and i could've drank ten of them, but i want to save some money while i am here. there was a mother and two kids in there that walked in about ten minutes after me. i could tell she had money. her daughter was vibrant and her baby boy was super curious about the trash can. as i sat down to eat, they got into their mercedes and drove away. i wonder what it's like driving one of those? i wonder what it's like having her for a wife? there is a different something about blondes.

i am betting on myself finally. i am not afraid of what will happen or could happen. i am giving my life to the paper with a starving artist mindset. if i lose, at least i am doing something i love and being honest with who i am. if i win, the bullshit i've gone through will still be my driving force. i will forever be thankful for my hardships. without them, i wouldn't bleed black and blue or red and yellow or purple and orange or midnight and sunrise or truth and conviction.

you talked as if you had known me before. as if our hearts were birthed from the same star. as if we once lived in the same flesh. as if we had never been forgotten by those we once loved. as if there is no ending to the name we share. as if there is a bigger place to rest our wings. you talked about life and i listened to every word that came out of you. i am a believer in who you are. no matter where we go throughout our life, i will stand, walk, and be beside you at every dead-end road we make our own.

maybe all we will ever be are a few pictures in a photo album covered with stained glass on a shelf for no one to see. for we will be the only ones who'll notice them when we need to be reminded of who were before we forgot how to talk to one another with a kind tongue. life is cruel and we become infatuated with pain once we have lived a little. we are curious creatures, with a set of eyes that see something different each time they are taken out in public. maybe we will fill the album with love instead of burning it along with the house we once made unforgettable.

i guess there is always someone in the relationship who
wants it more than the other. i just thought i would be
the one who cared when it turned out to be you.

i just thought it would matter to me more than it did.
i just thought i would be devastated by the fact that
you screwed me over. but after the rain had fallen,
i pulled up a chair and listened to it with a sound
i hadn't heard before. i listened to it without you
trying to drown it out.

i always wondered what it would feel like to lose something

you never had. it hurts even more when you were never

meant to hold it to begin with.

i really did want this to work, but love isn't supposed to be this fucking difficult. i wasn't a fool for coming out here. i was an idiot to believe in you. but with my trip, i have learned where i need to be and what i need to be doing and who i should have been loving all this time.

so, thank you.

i didn't stay for you. i needed to be away from everything
a little longer and soak in the light this wondrous place has
given to me. it is a writer's paradise being here. it is my own
piece of universe that even without you, has felt like home.
i needed to recharge, and now i am loaded with all the tools
that will carry me far away from you. a place where i can be
safe and accountable for who i choose to be. a place that has
nothing you've ever touched or breathed in. something of
my own where i can remain happy and carefree without
your eyes lying to me.

she kept me away from my demons long enough to see how beautiful things can feel once you have someone to protect you from anything causing you pain. i've learned to appreciate the darkness as much as the silence in the light, but with her, the moans and whispers do just fine.

this was the third chance i gave you and each time it has fucked me over worse than the previous one. but like with most painful things, it all ends eventually. it all ends and you begin to actually live for the first time without having to worry if they love you, because you finally learned how to value worth, instead of lust.

no one will ever tell me who to be again. i allowed their

lies to damn near ruin me, and now, i am free falling into

an open world full of love and serendipity. jump out of

your skin for the life you want. it is a wild, wild place

once you do.

i took my heart out to shine and dust the rust off. it had

been dormant for too long and it needed the magic around

me to beat for something real and raw again. something i

knew would return the love i had given.

i believe the power of positivity exists. you must believe and think about what you want. you must sacrifice possibly your life or a decent portion of it to become great and to have meaning injected into your soul. without those things, you are an empty body filled with "could-have-beens" and "should-have-beens."

there's a lot to figure out about who you are before you turn thirty. i am still learning and admiring those older than me, wondering how they did it and progressed through their lifetime. it's where my fascination with humans started. when i was a kid, i always gravitated towards my grandparents or anyone else older than my mom or dad. they might not have always had the answers, but they could bullshit you the truth if needed be. there is a connection i feel to them. it is as if we are the same age, just with different experiences. there's nothing greater than hearing a story about wwi, wwii, or the great depression to get your perspective about your own problems. find time to listen to the elderly. they didn't make it this far without picking up a few trade secrets to share. they are here for us. learn to respect that and then respect will find you.

i am slowly making my way towards being who i needed when I was struggling to find my direction. it is not the easiest thing to do, reteaching yourself the past in a sober manner. but i can tell how much of the alcohol i abused and how little i enjoyed just having a single drink. i have always for the most part been a complicated human with a love for the simplistic side of life. i am a paradox of the highest degree when tested. i drank to remember just as much as i did to forget. i always hated waking up hungover and still drunk from the night before, but it would only be a few hours before i restarted the process of drinking more than anyone to be someone entirely different each time. learning how to be sober during this day and age is taxing to say the least. with the constant onslaught of commercial use and peer pressure, it is as if they want us all to be alcoholics just for the sake of money and validation for their brand. i choose to be myself. i choose to run with lions and wolves instead of having the leftovers from hunters who only kill for sport.

time slowed down just enough that i found my bones under me. i found my footing and soul. i found who no one ever wanted to get to know because of who i was. time slowed down today and it has been for a while. it makes you value the days a little more. it makes you value the people who actually stay when the party is over and the entertainment has left just so they can ask if you are okay and if you need anything. those are my people. those are my constellations of truth and direction. it is how i guide myself to the next set of moments that will inspire me and direct me to a location in need of a helper.

i wrote a book about you. it isn't based on anything we did, because you never had any time to spend with me. this is my diary of what you did to me and how you allowed me to feel heartbroken over something you never fucking gave a damn about in the first place. i guess there is always one person who has to suffer for the betterment of a life. aren't you lucky i can write poetry now?

i have been free from any kind of burden for almost two weeks now. of course i still have a life and bills to pay and taxes to submit when i get home, but this was worth the price i have paid physically and literally. i hiked mountains i probably won't ever get to again. i spent a few hours in sin city with my little brother. i hung my feet off of the dixie rock. i left notes for others at pioneer park. i have walked this city every day looking for something i didn't see before. i've gone to town square park three times to sit with locals. i have driven almost two thousand miles since i left texas twelve days ago. my new jeep has gotten to live it with me. i am paying my own phone bill now. i have my own phone. i got two new tattoos since i have been here at alpha and omega by an artist named adrain. the sun has looked different each day and the moon seems to get closer every night. sure my bank account took a hit, but my life is better.

the sun sinks below the horizon again, with hopes of making someone else's day better by giving love and energy it develops through the travel. a small kiss on the mountains, and it is gone again. it leaves a warm patch for others as they go walking through the night. as i look out to the west, the image of the pristine mountainside and single tree will forever be burned into my mind. each ray, branch, and colored stone will be leaving with me as i aim to make something for myself. as i try to give hope to those who need it as much as i did when i first got here and they greeted me with the kindest and surest form of love.

i thought i came here for a single purpose, but it turned out my life was aching for something else entirely. for a time i thought the ocean was my true love, turns out this city and environment i have been subjected to, was all i needed to see to know it was never mine to begin with. nothing ever truly is. we are merely passing through and loan out all the things we care about hoping to have it returned better than it was found. hoping someone actually gives a shit about it as much as we have fought for it to remain with us and a part of us.

i am ready to get back and do the things i need so i can start on the next few books. plus i want to see if i can carry and maintain this lifestyle back home and what else i need to work on to make what i want a reality. it has been therapeutic being away from everyone. it has given me time to put value on my own life and allow me the space i need to create and figure out what is best for myself. i don't need someone looking over me. i don't need another mother or father. i need more love, art, and my ever growing thoughts on life in general. i really am happy on my own. being around other humans, they tend to make a mess of what you are putting together. i don't pretend to need anyone, because it has been this way a large portion of my life. i was raised by loneliness and embraced by change. what i am looking for has no walls or boundaries. it simply floats and maintains its structure by committing to whatever it loves.

it will be easier this way. we never got to hang out so i don't know what missing you feels like. i hope i never do. it is a feeling many are familiar with; missing what you have grown to have in your life. i am thankful you have never been more than a distant someone to me. someone who lived here but never loved. someone who was so scared of being with another human because it would mean you would have needed to change. that is not the life for you, and i am ecstatic it wasn't a life with you.

i hope when people look at my scars and tattoos, they see a story and not judge me because i am different. if they do, and chances are they will, maybe i can take out a sheet of paper and write them something without knowing anything about them. it may freak them out more, but maybe they will see value in words the same way i see it in flesh and honesty. the same way i see them is how i wish to always be seen and loved and appreciated; simply and full of mistakes.

little kids swimming in the indoor pool. denny's worker
on a smoke break. burger king worker on a smoke break.
cars passing through the street. everyone living their own
life within fifty yards of the other and each one living and
doing something they love, hate, or have no other options
left besides doing it. the workers look around before going
back in. the little girl looks at her parents and then holds
her breath and breaks the water. rushing to the top,
she looks at her parents for approval. the two workers
look at no one and go back at it for a few more hours.
all living. all dying the same way.

i wonder if anyone is observing me and writing what they see in a journal or note section on their phone the same way i am with those around me? i wonder if they saw me eat my last handful of trail mix for the night? i wonder if they can see my new tattoos when i step out on the balcony? i wonder if they see my jeep and notice the texas plates and wonder if i am some kind of cowboy? i wonder if they saw the arizona, idaho, and california plates in the parking lot? i wonder if they can hear this typewriter or my thoughts more clearly? i wonder if they wonder about the oddities of life.

it has been such a treat being able to leave my door

open as often as i have. you never quite know what

kind of life is going to walk in. you never know

what kind of nightmare will leave.

she doesn't wear shoes that often. she barely wears
her clothes, but she is comfortable in her earthly and
motherly state. she loves the natural feel of the universe
beneath her toes. she loves feeling the sun in the morning,
knowing it is another chance to make what didn't happen
yesterday, happen today. she is a case of wine that you savor
for the day after the actual celebration just to enjoy yourself.
she never is ready on time, but she is always ready for the
next adventure should one ever come her way.

i want to be a good role model for kids. i may cuss too much. i may have too many tattoos. i may have ugly scars. i may do a lot of things in an unnatural way, but i live it the best i can. i want kids to see it all and know they can still make something out of their lives and have something they can be proud of after it has all been taken away from you. i want them to know my struggles with addiction so they know it can be a positive impact on your life and not hinder you from your goals should they ever fall victim to that side of being human. i want them to know about my DUIs so they can see it never stopped me from getting my license back and to teach them how not to act. i want them to know i tried to kill myself so they know it never has to get to that point before asking for help. i want them to know i live with my father so they know you aren't worthless if you end up there longer than you thought.
i want them to read my words and feel comfort in knowing i have gone though it all in order to teach them it's okay to fuck up as long as you don't allow it to define you.

i have caught stars with my phone, and yet, it still feels like us humans have so much to learn from our ancestors above us. how we never take time to realize a moment until it is no longer around for us to enjoy. how we rarely take time for those around us until it is too late to enjoy their company the next time. i am realizing how much of my life i have turned in before making it better than what was given to me. i need to be a better human. that is what i will be working towards in my next chapter of living. in my next twenty-four hours.

i don't know what keeps me up more,
the thought of not writing enough or
not giving you the love you need.

both are focal points in my life.
having one without the other
throws off my axis, and on those
days, i cannot help but to walk
sideways with the sun.

i often think of the moon as a human light.

    she is calm when the rage is real.
    she is present long after everyone
    leaves. she makes sure you are
    loved in every phase and not just
    when full. the truth is, she remains
    full regardless of where you are,
    because she too had to learn how
    to be without the things she loves.

stephen hawking died today. it saddens me to see legends go. he was seventy-six and they said he went peacefully at his home in cambridge. he made the universe gnarly to speak of and made you think as einstien did when he was creating his theories. mr. hawking was a pioneer before anyone believed in him. some looked at him and saw nothing more than a wheelchair. but i promise you, he did more in that chair than others ever will standing on two feet. he not only talked in a celestial way, he was one of our brightest ones to have ever existed. may he go back home and be with the stars and universe for always.

i was only free when i stopped chasing what my heart wanted, and followed yours instead. the only thing i knew, was that the evil in the world would never touch you as long as i was with you. i will follow you into whatever feeling or place you need to be. i will follow you through it all if it means being able to keep loving you. and when i need to, i will take your hand and allow you to follow me.

i love, love. it has shown me its deepest fears and we have

traded secrets we will keep forever. i love, love. it hurts so

goddamn good and gives you the morning feels and the

night vibes. i love, love. it only asks everything from you.

that's pretty fucking rare.

i closed my blinds and felt the bed turn back
for me. it's calling my name, but i am still
making love to this typewriter. such a love/hate
relationship we have with the things that beg for
our attention.

tomorrow is my last full day here. it will be wednesday again here in this city. hard to believe time doesn't even stop for you when you finally find your eyes. funny how much you look back at your years and can pinpoint the exact moment your soul was unearthed under a pile of nothingness you had been told you were. it's funny how ignorant humans are when it comes to a life that's not their own. it's why i don't and won't ever get a long with my fellow walkers.

all the "poets" nowadays think she is something new every day. they think she is the only way to sell books. if you sell your soul first then maybe, but the best seller of all time won't amount to shit if they are writing blind to begin with. clear your heart and clean your mind. scratch and claw words out. edit the entire page.i don't know about you, but i am fond of clean, breathable, and healthy air, as well as a clean, breathable, and healthy book.

look down. look up. look beyond the sun. look where no one else is. keep looking until your eyeballs land on the magic they know is out there. once you find it and you feel yourself needing to blink, do so without fear of losing sight of it again. magic always returns to those who believe.

doing your best is only worth the sweat

you put into it. occasionally it will be

mixed with blood and confusion, but if

you remain on this path, you will drink

with the gods.

i will never understand those who do not get up to see the
sunrise or walk out to see the sunset. i am in love with both.
it is the truest infatuation my body has known. how can
something so beautiful exist in such a toxic place at times?
there is nothing better than seeing those two things to begin
and end my day. there was a man sitting in his truck earlier.
he walked over to the store to get a cup of coffee and is in
the parking lot watching the same thing i am with just as
much enthusiasm. that's what life is about. getting out
of your skin to view the impossible, the unexplainable,
to know something greater is out there for us.

it's so quiet here this morning. i can hear the birds in my

head and feel them nesting and feeding their young. i can

hear them sing a morning song, an ambitious calling to the

rest of the wildlife inhabiting my thoughts.

denny's is beginning to fill up. humans needing their grease
and caffeine. three construction workers sit outside of their
vehicles and eat breakfast biscuits from the convenience
store. they lift the hood to check the oil and fluids then
shut it promptly and start bullshitting about their night.
we all have our routines and we all need something in
the morning to get us going. for some, it is food. others
it's coffee. for another few it is sex. the rest are just trying
to figure out why they are up so early.

a husband and wife leave the burger king with food being carried in his hands and a cigarette in hers. most of the people vape out here. seems to be the way to go when trying to be healthy. this is only the third smoker i have seen, and in some ways, it is odd to see it. this place is clean and pure for those who live here. you have your motorcycles, monster trucks, and hybrids. such a paradox being here, but it takes that to be different. to have your own personality. i don't judge others. i simply observe, feel, and translate it all. i am a messenger with infinite emotions and personalities. i, too, am a paradox. hence why i don't want to leave.

i mute the tv to hear nature. to hear human activity. to hear the sounds of the earth around me asking for its patience and recognition. it is the only time i give my full attention. it is the only time no one ever bothers me with news about the world. in some ways, i am an asshole, but excuse me for enjoying my earth time.

no longer am i afraid of what could happen. for i am too

busy mapping out what will happen. i hold my own life in

my hands. i hold my own truth in my heart. i hold my next

fifty years in the promise to give each breath its own voice

and for that to carry me through to somewhere i belong.

the maids here know little english, but they are always
smiling. even if you're having a shitty day/morning, they
walk into your life knowing nothing about you, but still
smile as if they are lucky to be alive and have their job.
i make my bed every morning, but leave it just enough
unmade so they can feel better about doing their job.
if they can get up with happiness exploding from their
eyes, then i can as well. i can't imagine the filth they
have to clean and the disgusting rooms some people
keep. i admire them for their effort. i admire them
for making money to help further their lives. i admire
them for saying good morning or hello, when you can
walk one hundred feet without anyone acknowledging
you. they don't do it because they have to. they do it
because they know hard work begins before you get up.

i have gotten by with stones for fingers and glass for eyes. i have gotten by with grass growing on my feet and the ocean swirling inside of me. i am more hurricane than earthquake. i am more unsure about love, but positive it is there for the taking. i am made of arrowheads and bamboo. all constructed and dismantled until i configure the perfect fit. it is damn near impossible when your head is holding your heart and your chest contains your mind.

i couldn't imagine waking up and doing something for thirty or forty years the same as everyone else. i won't ever have millions or hundreds of thousands of dollars, but i will have my outlook on life and appreciate how we all make a living doing something we love or hate. we do it because we have to or need to. i never want to be that person who has to just because. i need fucking conviction or else i'm wasting my life and everyone else's time and energy. i am a man searching for substance, searching for the truth of why we are who we are, and why so many keep living the same life for all these years, when it only takes a day to change you.

not knowing anything about my future has given
the strength to walk away satisfied with my effort
and feeling thankful the heart only breaks for
humans who share the same pain as they do when
the ache splits them down the middle of the soul.
luckily, i have remained whole and alive. i am still
here and walking to my next adventure without
having to carry the baggage you left me with at the
door. alone i'll go and alone i'll be, but together i
am and together i'll breathe.

i don't know what i will miss the most when i leave.

i am not going to dwell on it too long. life is not

guaranteed to us tomorrow, so i will give my best

effort to this day. to this feeling, now.

i am leaving tomorrow morning and will be

taking with me new bones, new flesh, new

life skills. that is all we can ask for when you

have been given everything you need by the

nature around you.

it's lunch time around here. drive throughs are getting backed up. angry humans not getting their fast food fast enough. anxious children causing their parents more stress than they can handle. the smell of hunger is real and with that, comes crazy road rage and horns beeping to move forward in line. i wish more people had time to go inside and eat or take their food outside and enjoy the scenery. the only ones who do, have already been living sixty plus years or more and understand the value of a minute.

i am starving for more adventure. the hunger pains keep me homesick and without knowledge of where i am needed. i point my heart to the next piece of road that my tired are begging to kiss and i allow them to stay connected where they are needed. my feet are unsteady. my hands keep tapping the keys in hopes of writing something never before read, something never before found. i write until all that's left is shedding skin and new fingernails from my growth as a human. the sun is beckoning me to come out to play. i am ready to journey around it again to get a better look at the man behind the desk. the man behind these words. the man who knows nothing..

being here has taught me how to be more
present and active in my own life. it has
showed me as long as your feet are moving
and your mind is firing, you will forever be
a changed human each day you strive for
wholeness. you can make art and still
have time to be accountable for your
actions. what you do with those things
and how you prepare for it will be what
creates the mindset that anything you want,
you can have, as long as it comes with only
the best intentions. if you are doing
something based on something differently,
you will always be swimming with your head
under water trying to breathe.

don't dig your own grave and ask how you fell in. no one looking down at you will care enough to remove you from it. they will only ask where are the shovels. my fears may speak, but my truth still screams. during the night, before the dirt moves, there is this subtle way about the night. there is no noise to hear for you to know if you are ready to get up. there is no noise for you to know what to do. you just hope they left you enough room to climb out.

the wind is picking up and bringing the rain they had predicted. feels like it is the right time to adjust my sails and follow it home in the morning. it is a new day. a new vision. a new blessing. a new miracle. it is the sun shining on us all. it is the people taking to their opinions and beliefs. the only thing i know is that this venue has more stars than worries.

this place has broken the glass around my heart. no longer does it read, "fragile." now it reads, "free." intimacy is my language. the strongest of humans know the most pain and have exited through the gates of hell a few times to give you a glimpse of what the other-side could be like if you learn to love them for who they are and not where they have been. may your wings never taste defeat.

people think you have to travel to experience
new things and write and find inspiration.
if you open your door and don't find it there,
then you will need to go elsewhere. boredom
with anything stiffens any production, and it
is a sad thing seeing another human dying as
they stay in a home that has wilted from within.

i've never been more sure of my path as i see it now. after all the setbacks and immature decisions, i have finally grown into the man i always knew i could be once i gave myself a chance to succeed. it took losing more than i've gained, but even an empty heart can produce love when it is given enough light in a new place.

i go outside and walk the balcony to see if i can notice anything different about where i am at. to feel the wind at different angles. to breathe in the smell of the trees and the blossoms budding on them. to envision my whole life here. i see it all vividly and my goosebumps stand and give a warm welcome to the potential that lives within the view from this hotel and the excitement bursting from my fingertips. it all works, and probably will have a few bad days, but i will trade those in to feel this swelling of happiness taking place today, and the days before.

being here for this long without you,
i forgot you even live here. i forgot
why i came out here and learned why
i am here. funny how the universe sends
us places and people in an attempt too
catch our attention by using something
entirely better and useful than feelings
and wishful thinking.

i need to understand how to stop giving my heart to those who don't know what to do with it or to those who can't hold it the way i need it to be held. life gets much simpler once you begin to listen to your own pain. maybe life is just reliving your past until you learn how to move on with it all and become your own reason for needing to let go.

i just saw an older couple walk out of burger king and the man walked his wife to the car, opened her door, walked around to his side still with the drinks and food in his hands. there is effort for us to see as a society, a chivalry to uphold, yet i see it every day, more and more care less about the ones they love and give it to themselves instead. i hope they enjoy their burger and shake. i hope when they get homer, he opens the door for her and they talk about the last forty years of their life together. they still get out of the house. they still go on dates. he still walks 4with her and wears her as if she is the most priceless and precious diamond. he isn't scared to have his love displayed for the world to see. he just does it. he does it because their generation before him put such a premium on love, they actually tried to get better at it each day, and not when they felt like it. it saddens me to see the downfall this new age society has produced. though there are those who still love like the nineteen-thirties, not many love with the same attention to detail.

it has been one of those trips you read about as a kid

and can't wait to be a part of. and like when you were

a kid, the days tend to go by to fast to remember

anything but the ending. even so, this will be

beautiful long after i am aged past my prime.

we are so scared to admit what we want that by the time

we do, everything we wanted is gone and we are left asking

where did the years go. where does the human heart hide

when the things it needs the most are the memories we

never have the nerve to capture.

we go out on adventures knowing we never want to

leave. no matter how good your life is now, nothing

will ever feel as good as when you first found it.

and that's what we spend the rest of our lives

trying to find. that first time feeling, again.

the workers from this morning are back after working their ten hour day. they check their tools, trucks, tires, and themselves as they trade in their work life for their home life. hopefully they did good enough to make it another day. hopefully they made enough to inch closer to that new home or vehicle they were talking about with their family. from the looks of their current situation, i'd say they are thankful to have what they have. and i am thankful this hotel has a guest laundry mat or else i would not value a fresh day as much as i do now. amazing what things we take for granted and what we ultimately cannot live without.

i went down seven minutes early to get my laundry and put it in the dryer. i was seven minutes early and noticed an old man with a utah basketball jacket on and he was using a walker to get around. the rain started as soon as i opened the door to check on my clothes. the rain smells fresher here. as if it came from the mountain springs themselves. it's colder, but damn does it feel revitalizing once it hits you. it dropped five degrees within seven minutes and i had just enough quarters to work the dryer. seven quarters in seven minutes. a lot can change in that amount of time. even the way you see someone you know nothing about.

i am gone in the morning and back to my own reality, but back to things i love to do and the things that provided me the ability to make this trip in the first place. i have learned a lot in the past twelve days. more so than i did in the eight years. i am able to be on my own without the assistance anyone. i can touch thunder and hear lightning. i can wake up and eat my breakfast without having to rush it into my mouth with fear of being late for a place or person that doesn't exist. i can use both lungs to breathe and use both hands to hold onto and let go of what i need. i can smile and not worry ab out the reason. which if you know me, that is all you need to know.

we oftentimes check and then double check to make sure we have what we already know we have. whether it be keys, wallet, phone, or whatever else before leaving the house or drive way. we do this so we can mentally check it off of our list and to give ourselves meaning in a normal routine. we want to know that we matter and that we are important. we need validation and approval at any given minute because we forget to check ourselves before leaving to go some place we either don't want to go or have no other choice but to go. we pride ourselves on being original though we continually forget we already are.

i feel you in my skin and between my breaths. you don't just

live in me, you are me before you were, you. we love being

connected. we love to be loved. we are us before the universe

gives us a place to call our own.

maybe i cured myself or maybe being here did.
whatever it was, my face feels like it has been
kissed by every star in the sky and i am complete.
not only in mindset, but spirit. as the rain continues
to fall and the thunder rocks around me, i remember
how it feels to be one with the outside world where
everything loves to relax and let it all fall down.

the palm trees dance as if every single dollar bill had been

thrown at them. they dance for no one, but they move for

the rain. they know people are watching, so they put on a

show for the onlookers. before it is over, everyone is broke

and mad to the bone.

be able to love yourself enough to where you aren't selling

who you are for someone you're not. if they don't love you

as is, they will never love what comes after it.

being here has shown me that if i want to, i can always come back. i can always come back to this feeling, this moment, this vibe, whenever i need it. i am leaving here with pieces of utah scattered across parts of nevada, new mexico, arizona, and texas. i was a born traveler, and travel will.

i'm not sure i have ever hated anyone as much as i loathe you. i sincerely hope you find whatever sorry soul you're looking for. maybe i am lucky things didn't work out. maybe i was meant to be here without ever seeing you. if i had, i wouldn't know how vindicated feels by leaving on my own terms.

i have written almost five hundred pages of the best work for me to date. it took traveling almost fourteen hundred miles to find who i was aching to be and to discover the life i was begging the universe for. i jumped and landed in a soft and forgiving place. it has cared for me and given me unconditional love. i will miss this place immensely, but i will have stories to tell others when i meet the ones who are meant to be in my life. i am filled with keys and ribbon. i can walk and talk in font. i left as a human and came back as a more seasoned writer.

i will miss the sunsets and sunrises the most. being out here, each one birthed an new though. each one gave me a new light. each one danced with my shadows and threw confetti upon this great city as i walked through the streets being my own hero. i was never alone while i was here. the sun and moon both guided my feet when they needed to walk and when they needed to rest. i will miss these sunsets and sunrises. i will miss the taste they gave my soul and it is something that will fuel me for many years to come. i will come back and they will know my name. they will know my secrets. they will know who they created if not already, i hope they do.

people will talk about their best days and some will read about their worst ones. i am a fan of life and everything that conspires into making us who we are. from the down and outs, to the homeless on the streets, to the waitress looking for that extra ten dollar tip to pay her rent, we are all sacrificing our best, just to end up as far away as we can from the worst. as long as we are helping one another as much and as often as we can. maybe we will all reap the reward of being a noble man or woman, living for something greater than what we we end up settling for.

we don't always understand why things happen the way they do. we are told it is a part of life and you cannot see the pain of everyone you meet. but in this instance, you could see her beauty, smile, and laughter. she had a different vibe of freedom to her. she had this infectious energy that once you were around her, you never doubted the earth you were standing on. dana was what we call a beautiful soul. someone who could transform the environment around her to create the magic we oftentimes couldn't find on our own. standing up here today and looking out over the room, we all have our demons. others hide them too well and let them out however they can, and then some simply cope with being a prisoner to them. dana was not a prisoner. she was her own person and wherever you go after today, i hope she stays with you forever. there aren't humans like her that come around this place that often and we should cherish the time we have with one another each day we are gifted. i hope you leave here knowing how much she loved you all and fought every day for another breath to share with those she loved. she lived her life the way she wanted and smiled all the way through it. today, an angel has left us, but her spirit remains inside of those she touched. dana was a warrior and someone who never lived in regret nor did she worry about what people thought of her. her life will not be measured by the abrupt ending of it, but by how long her name will live on throughout the walls we walk, beaches we stroll, and laughs we share knowing how much love lived inside of one woman.

> *-i wrote this for a woman i never knew, for a family that reached out to me. i was honored to have been able to do this for them-*

we don't always understand why things happen the way they do. we are told it is a part of life. you cannot see the pain of everyone you meet. but in this instance, you could see her beauty, smile, and laughter. she had a different vibe of freedom to her. she had this infectious energy that once you were around her, you never doubted the earth you were standing on. someone who could transform the environment around her to create the mystic we oftentimes couldn't find on our own. we consciously and subconsciously tuck away our demons. others let them out however they can, and then some simply cope with being a prisoner to them. she lived her life the way she wanted and battled all the way through it. she's a warrior and someone who never lived in regret nor did she worry about what people thought of her. her life will not be measured by the abrupt ending of her fairy tale, because someone like her builds a legacy that will live on throughout the walls we walk, beaches we stroll, and the immense love which lived inside of one woman.

-the edited version of the one i wrote for dana and her family-

then i fell upon the grass to hear you breathe. i felt each rotation you were moved by. i felt each inhale your sweet lungs could take. i felt the name the cosmos gave you before your skin was covered in the star-like freckles creating lines for my fingers to trace. i felt the moon sigh the first time you flew. i felt the love only spoken by true believers of the word. it is here with us, and here it will keep us safe.

and they both arrived together under the same sky.
where life gives you lessons disguised as humans.
where life gives you a place to make your own.
where life gives you loss to show you acceptance
of the mortality we all face. where life gives you
friendship to create a bond that will get you
through your worst days when you feel like the
ground beneath you is giving way to the hell you
have read about. but you won't live this life lonely.

i know my purpose lies beyond this day. that's what keeps me going. it is the stumbling which allows me to learn my feet and legs and how incredibly agile they are when you know what you are after. it is the letting go which promises me something better to attach my fingers and palms to when they being loosening. when they release what was only meant to be a brief moment of acceptance. there is a mighty calling to us all, and may you rummage through the madness to find yours.

vulnerability is the most exhilarating form of living.

if someone cannot be vulnerable with me then it's

not a friendship i want. transparency is where life is

made and lost. i respect those who can be that with

anyone they meet.

we want to explore the possibility that something greater
is out there. we want to know that we aren't alone in our
feelings and emotional states. we want to eat new foods
and discover new origins of what makes everyone fall in
and out love. we at times choose to sit in peace and quiet
with only a few lights on above our heads and look out
windows and not care about what's going on around us.
i look out and see a sun bursting with laughter and a
palm tree waving at everyone as they go by it. it waves
to me, and i return the gesture.

-moon-

and there you are, never asking for anyone to look at you. you are a connection to the unexplainable. you are the fixation of all things beautiful and unknown. you are every bit of me as i am every bit of you. the parts of you that fall, land gently by my feet. as I collect them, i feel the pain they once carried and i send them back to you without expecting you to mend what hurts in me.
but you do it every single time.

some of us speak in light to get through the darkness. our eyes have never been open long enough to value the sights we miss. to value the colors that make up the universe we live in. to value the human side of regret. to value the unmistakable truth of growing up blinded by the false pretense of everything is not made for us. everything is ours. we just need to leave them open before running into something else that tells us differently.

if you never look up, you will miss the best parts of life. from the satellites crossing stars. to the milky way reminiscing her glory days to orion. to the sureness the sun loves with. to the abilities of thought perpetrated by the moon during her fullness of laughter. there is such an array of larger scope ideas and ideals to be had when witnessing what you know nothing about, or thinking you know it all. it all lights up the blood running wildly around your core.

and tomorrow we will try again to find more words,
more feelings, more moments. and tomorrow we
will find a way to develop a better sense of self.
a more reliable ally than staying broken. a more
resolve for the problems in our lives. a more
directed approach to living instead of pretending
to use the strings tied to our limbs to move forward.

look at everything with an open soul.
we are all susceptible to the agony
we feel, create, and harbor. do not
allow the current to take you.
we hold more than a heart inside.
we are made of more than just fragility
others use against us. once you see
yourself as more than a distilled human
dancing around naked and shapeless,
you will come to know a plentiful supply
of hope and love.

we should want more than what we have, but not at

the cost of losing who we are. be wildly optimistic.

be incredibly adventurous. be the reason you get

up and want more. fear is only there for you to

find yourself and a broken heart can still be loved

if you are still in search of something meaningful.

-sunsets-

and then it slowly brings you back to the beginning.
before the mind killed you. before the heart deceived
you. before the hands forgot the touch of love.
before the lips caught wind of betrayal. before it all,
a wondrous creation was made to see you through
the chaos. i believe in my own version of heaven and
hell. i believe in the synchronicity around us and how
everything demands to be felt. i believe in the power
of a sunset changing your life. i have seen too many
not to.

if you don't chase after your dreams, that's all they will ever be. there are unmarked graves where they go to die and never to be visited again. they are left to rot with the rest of the earth you never saw. they remain there buried and alone. they are there withering deeper into the confines of a hole you loved more than a better life. someone probably told you one time nothing ever comes true, and you believed them.

you must be willing to do the impossible if it means making anything else possible in your life. it means getting up after you promised yourself you would never stay down. it means getting out of bed despite the immense pain cemented around your heart. it means taking a chance on the job you feel unworthy of having. it means breathing in deeper, teaching your lungs to breathe in the fire. it means taking a few minutes more each day to care for the lonely living in your soul. it means finally finding a way out of the crazy and into something more maddening to fight for. it means being okay even when you are not. sometimes we have to tell ourselves it will be before anyone else gives a damn. and if you are the kind of person who never looks for someone's approval, prove it to the man or woman or child you are. life goes better when you are at least honest with the promise of something more to live for.

where you are has always been where you've needed to be. the art. the music. the pain. the ache. the loss. the unknown. all of it makes you, human. we don't understand until we are mature enough to handle it, but the wild in us has been too much for those who have never experienced life. those who are afraid of the image they see in the mirror. those who are scared of the adventure. take comfort in what you so and where you are. this is never the ending of a journey. it is merely the start of a new day.

to be alone you must first be able to handle the domain of your own mind. you must remember it isn't always acting in your best interests. there are games we all encounter when trying to be someone we aren't for the sake of having a future. there is no such thing as losing when you are fucking trying to make your reality more homely.

life is nothing more than loving yourself when no one else can. we are the greatest love story there is. each individual consists of beautiful parts of every place they have ever been. unfortunately for some, some of those same places involved someone who ruined them for the rest of the world. to be at peace with who you are, you must first take time to adore those parts before moving on with your life. before the heart formally meets the soul, you must.

there is a life out there for you. i hope you have the strength to make it beautiful. i hope you have the guts to stand up for what it is you need. i hope you have enough self-respect to know what you should never settle for. i see too many faces who pretend to shine with the sun who are full of the dark matter we try to rid from ourselves. the prettiest aren't always the happiest. the most confident aren't always the ones you should follow. be humble in your journey, but do not take any shit from those who see you as a threat. they should never take your time or energy when it comes to living.

i am only concerned about myself and will continue to
do what i need to so i can keep it that way. i had been
self-sacrificing for over ten years and that time has came
and went. i am ready for the challenges ahead of me.
my affirmations are solely based on my comprehension
of who i need and who will never serve me purpose.
me, myself, and i are the main focus at this moment.
one day i will try again to have a group worthy of
being a part of. for now though, i have to be this
way to maximize my talents and heartiness.

i deal with depression, anxiety, and ptsd every day. some days are better than others, but i haven't really had a bad one in years. i am a recovering addict. i am a suicide survivor. i am a human. my pain has allowed me to become myself even if i tried to end it all. i am still here and i thank you all for opening your souls to my work. i should be dead but i am not, so i will keep doing what makes me happy and love every single fucking minute, including the pain.

no matter where my life takes me or the amount of stress
and unknown is out beyond me, i know you are there.
i know you are as close as the stars are to the moon even
on the nights when she feels alone and crying inconsolably.
there is this way about you. one that time and space cannot
contain or describe. i always picture my days with you and it
is what keeps the magic flowing through my heart.

let love be a part of your life. let your own love be the driving force. too often we feel obligated to involve someone else when in fact, all that is needed is a kind of revalation, a mind-blowing instance to occur to become our true-selves. i hope you find it without having to go into to hell. i hope you find it on the corner of the your mind you haven't used in a while. the part segregated for lost memories and anger. whatever you find, may it be your story. may it be your lifeline. may it be your ever after.

love doesn't always stay. sometimes it is there just
long enough to teach you what you still need to
learn. sometimes it is there without you ever
seeing it. the beauty comes before the pain.
the rain comes before the storm. the flowers
sing before the night. the trees grow before
they are planted. the smell of summer begins
during the winter months where everything tends
to be a reminder of what once was and what may
never be again. but it all comes back to us. we all
remember why we laugh and never forget why it did.

if you leave, don't ask me how i am doing. if you didn't want my love, i am not giving you my friendship. it is simple when it comes to my trust. if I cannot see you in my future, your presence in present is not a gift at all. it is showcasing why i changed and why you never you did.

when you figure out how you want your life to be, don't

allow someone to interrupt your path by giving you reasons

why it won't work. some of us choose to be those around us,

while some of us choose to be what we are. there are better

ways to waste your time.

your acceptance for what i do has zero impact on how i live my life. the things i love are the same things you will never understand. it's not a slight against you. you just cannot see the world as i do, and that's okay, but you will not tell me who i should be in order to be accepted.

maybe one day you will know how long i have waited to be only yours. maybe before the bones give way and the soul is set free. maybe before i even say another word about how much i have missed you and how you know all the places where i go to hide. maybe before this even finds you, you will know who you are to me and why i have remembered you as if you were the first kiss i ever had and will ever need to know.

your worth will always be determined by the way you see yourself. it is something no one else can see. it is something no one else can prove no matter how much they know you. there is a sacrifice to be had once you figure it out. some will leave your life because they want and others will leave because you tell them. not everyone you meet is supposed to know the real you all your life. they are there to teach you who you don't have to be in the end and still know happiness is not a feeling, but an approach to the life you want.

not everything is going to make sense to you. it is up to us to

find the things we love that do not need an explanation. you

just need to feel it. be mindful when assisting your growth as

a human.

never allow someone to make you feel unworthy just because they aren't happy with who you are. they will never be content with anyone who isn't kneeling for them. some of us carry the sword and others are the sword. find a way to be both and you will discover the true meaning of being capable of fighting your own battles and finishing the wars.

whatever you do today, don't settle for what you don't want. as we all know, life is painfully short for a lot of us who wish to have a better life. do not wait until you are at your very end to decide on something better. even if you begin there, at least you are willing to embrace a change many go without until they are writing things down for their children or parents to read aloud at their own services.

be thankful for the pain. it is teaching you how to master the art of humility. knowing we aren't alone in our suffering beings about a certain clarity we crave. we are the dust before it settles and the foundation before the house is built. all the experiences we go through, shape our future. if the snow has the privilege to hear your smile, i hope the rest of the seasons get a chance to as well.

be in the moment now. don't miss an opportunity to embrace the details of something beautiful that might not be there tomorrow. if you are to bet on the chances of something normal ever staying in your life, you must accept the fact that change is inevitably around each corner you fold back.

some people just love too much and that's why they hurt for so long. do not wait until the last time to say how you feel. all of this is just temporary. we only get to feel the fire once. even if it doesn't work out, finding you has been the most wildest and unexpected adventure of my life. and if you do anything, go wild for a while. your existence is my love story. at the end of it all, you can endure all the tragedies and still come out of it as fresh as wildflowers.

make time for yourself and stop apologizing for the things you didn't cause. the only way to forgive, is to accept that it's not always your fault. you will never move on if you keep looking back. what's there has nothing to do with what you couldn't do. it has everything to do with who they couldn't be. you don't owe them anything. not even a second glance.

i don't know what to do most of the time, but when i feel

the need to create, i can spend days without human contact

and immersing myself in a place that doesn't quite yet exist,

but believing it will at some point during your journey.

make moves and get out of the situation that's dragging

you down. life is too short to be miserable without giving

yourself a chance to be happy. it is in the pain where you

will find who you really are. unfortunately, this comes at

a huge cost at your own well-being, but if you want

to come out of it healthy and whole, you must endure

what cannot be saved and find a way to move on.

life is truly the most fascinating part of the universe. it is all

we know and at times doesn't make sense. then there are

moments where it slaps us in the face with the softest form

of understanding and enlightenment.

the strongest connections happen a million miles away.

i write in hopes of you reading and finally seeing yourself

in my words. and like with all things precious, you must

allow space for love.

there is greatness within the breath you carry. each one has the potential to change a life. you will outlive the pain and become the magic so many humans need. being yourself is the bravest thing you can ever be. we weren't made to survive. we were made to be wild in life.

healing is not something others define for you.

it is your wound. you decide. you will find the

right people when you begin loving who you

are. no matter how bad it gets, we all can start

over after what we thought would never end.

the greatest thing you can do is give yourself a chance.
one day you will wake up and feel nothing. no more
anxiety. no more depression. no more excuses.
no more angst. just happiness for being here. i hope
you make it worth it. i hope it makes you able to love
again.

the soul knows love, because it is the purest form walking

in this crazy world. we die a little more each day without

the art we need. you never know what you're capable of

until someone breaks you and leaves you alone to pick up

the mess.

if you need to heal, take your time. don't fast track your own well being for someone who has never been through what you have. you aren't weak. you are being honest with who you are. if that's a problem for someone who says they care about you, they don't deserve you.

it's getting heavy. it's beginning to break the bones, but you

and i are set in stone. when it comes to anything related to

love, it is ready when you are. it is ready to wait out all of

the storms in your path, just so you can touch the sky one

more time.

laugh as often as you can. make memories that will take you

back to yourself when you are feeling lost. laugh your way

back to love. be somewhere that makes you happy with

someone who allows you to be yourself. wherever you

conceive your next journey, my you love the breath you

take to uncover it.

there are times in a single life where everything feels at peace and the ache is no longer attached to the bones we carry. we meet peace with open hearts and they are flooded with love. there are souls we come across and we hope to know where they came from so we can go back with them when it is time to lay down for a lifetime.

love is deeper than the roots of any star and it is there i will stay with you until we both fall back into the universe from a wish by ourselves we left behind. leave us be until we can see the seasons of the moon change for the sun.

||leave us there||

sit with me for a while and let's get lost in
thought of making it. better days await us.
you are them. you've always been my
sunrise and sunset, sweet one.

    be with someone who can hold you
    before you ever feel like falling. if it
    doesn't work out in your favor,
    may you learn how to fall gracefully
    and full of light.

we knew what we were doing, yet we found ourselves losing

it all each time we held each other, looking for a deeper

reason to give more than our bones and souls.

between your heart and stars is where life greets you.

it took a broken home. it took overcoming and still battling addiction. it took a failed suicide attempt. it took me eight years of my life since being out of the marine corps. it is an everyday struggle, but nothing has felt more rewarding than being able to write my own story. nothing has felt more rewarding than regaining my license after being without it for six years. self-love has never felt better than it does now. the beautiful thing about life, is that each human has stories that need to be told. i sincerely hope you can arrive to the place where you can share it, and still love yourself after it.

many times i have fallen. many times i never thought i'd be able to get up without leaning on my addiction to recover from it. i have spent more than half of my life running from who i was so i could feel normal for a day. i am not proud of any of it if i am being honest. i hated myself and everything i was connected to. i dreamt of the days where i could wake up not reaching for a bottle. i dreamt of days knowing i would be able to handle my own shit without needing an excuse to slip back into the darkness. i scared those i loved because i wasn't afraid of who they saw. today is different. it has been for a while now.

not everything has to be right in order to give your best
effort. i had been struggling for years and still am to a
degree, i didn't know where my life was going because
i couldn't see myself ever being happy. i couldn't see
all of what i had already accomplished. i am a
perfectionist. i am ocd about things others don't
notice or care about. over the last three years i have
been fortunate enough to find something i love to do
and will give everything i have to it in order for me to
succeed. we wander this place for a chance to be free in
every degree of the word. we care too much about certain
things and don't care enough about other stuff. my life
hasn't gone according to plan because i never planned
anything out. i don't operate that way. i live each day
as a singular stance in my pursuit of vibes and a calling.
i am a wanderer of tie and space. i am a ball of light
searching for something beyond this place. i don't
always have the perfect words. i just have feelings.

she looked at me with eyes made from moons of another world. she didn't know it then, but i had known her before when i was just a soul traveling across the universe to find shelter from the black holes. not everything needs a beginning to know how real and meaningful it all was. she gives me the reason to keep chasing after my own heart, when i am not consumed in trying to devour hers.

we don't always figure life out. sometimes we just need

to open our hearts to accept the universe. one day you

will have what they said you didn't deserve. one day

you will be where you've always wanted to be. one day

you will become your grandest adventure, and you will

have it all.

every once in a while we meet
someone who wants to know
why we hurt. pain seems to stop
for a brief moment and you begin
to feel lucky about everything you
are a part of.

now there is only an ache in that spot right in the middle of

my heart where you used to be. we hurt each other because

we thought love was what we wanted. ever since you, i do

not trust those who look up at the sky and feel nothing.

the only thing you ever showed me was how to walk away.

may the sun and moon both keep you safe and filled with adventures. love can only save those who will keep it safe. tell me the secrets your bones carry. not everything needs to make sense. it if makes you feel alive, love it, learn it, and breathe it all the way into your soul. give it the rest it was too scared to ask for and it will give you a life you were too afraid of seeking.

my biggest inspiration is pain. i have dealt with many over the years of life and i have come to find that love is the common denominator. we are given this life to wildly explore. anything less and you are missing out on your full potential. i found out later in life that it hurts because it wasn't supposed to be a lesson.

you may not be perfect to your own eyes, but i love the way you see yourself. you are beautiful and deserve all the stars. even the ones you thought had gone into hiding, preparing for the fall. the only way I knew how to love was by the way you held me.

|^|and like rain, you give me life|^|

sometimes i am. sometimes i am not. it is up and down for the most part, but happiness visits me at times and i am grateful for every moment that it decides to. how precious of a thought it is to know after all you have been through, it still cares in the end.

my heart matches your soul. just give me you forever.
i always feel like the luckiest when you share your
body with me. we are the moments we fought for
to have a beautiful life. the love you want is the love
you're willing to give. you are the symbol of my life
and the epitome of all things free.

you feel like the life i had been born to live.
if anything can change you, it is the first kiss.
you know it will either kill you or bring you
peace down the road. sometimes it will feel
like both and those are the moments i live
for with you now. it has been the most
extraordinary journey with you, and i
cannot wait to watch more sunrises and
sunsets with you at my side. where the
ocean meets the moon, that is our space
of infinity. open yourself up to new
sensations, new feelings, new possibilities,
new love, new skin. with each new breath,
our hearts find their fight.

to those who have a story to tell,
sing it out. to the ones who have
a dream, release it. to the ones
who have been broken, may you
find the light needed to shine
again. to the ones who feel like
the pain is too much, take that
next step and know it will be
okay. to the ones who are
scared of tomorrow, please,
live for today, and just breathe.

www.ingramcontent.com/pod-product-compliance
Lightning Source LLC
Chambersburg PA
CBHW032038290426
44110CB00012B/858